Wizard Balloon

First published in 2008
by Wayland

This paperback edition published in 2009

Text copyright © Anne Cassidy 2008
Illustration copyright © Martin Remphry 2008

Wayland
338 Euston Road
London NW1 3BH

Wayland Australia
Hachette Children's Books
Level 17/207 Kent Street
Sydney, NSW 2000

Series Editor: Louise John
Cover design: Paul Cherrill
Design: D.R.ink
Consultant: Shirley Bickler

A CIP catalogue record for this book is available from the British Library.

ISBN 9780750251853 (hbk)
ISBN 9780750251860 (pbk)

Printed in China

Wayland is a division of Hachette Children's Books,
an Hachette Livre UK Company

www.hachettelivre.co.uk

Wizard Balloon

Written by Anne Cassidy
Illustrated by Martin Remphry

WAYLAND

Wizard Wizzle wanted a magic
carpet more than anything.

He cast a magic spell.

The carpet flew up into the air. His sister Wanda was amazed!

Wizzle tried to grab the carpet but
it zoomed off.

"Oh dear!" he said.

The king came running over.

"Look!" he shouted. "The queen has given me a birthday present. It's a hot air balloon!"

The king, the queen and all the lords and ladies watched as the balloon landed on the ground.

10

"Wow!" said Wizzle, "I would love
to have a go in that!"

"Come for a ride with me, Wizard
Wizzle!" the king said.

"It could be dangerous!" said
Wanda. "Do be careful!"

"Well, a balloon won't zoom off
without me like that magic
carpet!" said Wizzle.

The balloon rose up into the sky.

It soared higher and higher.

"This is so much fun!" laughed
Wizzle. "Wanda looks really tiny!"

But the king was turning a funny colour. His face was green.

"It's too high!" he shouted, "I feel sick. I want to get out."

Wizzle looked in his book for a spell.

Wizzle took some magic owl feathers and a dragon's claw out of his pocket.

He put them into his hat, waved
his wand and shouted some
magic words.

"Izzle, Wizzle, Woo! Take us down
to the ground!"

There was a sparkle, a fizz and a puff of smoke.

The balloon began to turn... and twist... and spin. Wizzle felt dizzy.

"Stop! Rescue me!" the king shouted. The balloon was going much too fast.

Suddenly it stopped. The balloon
was stuck in the branches of
a tree!

"Oooh," gasped the queen and the lords and ladies.

But Wanda had an idea.

She began to climb up a
nearby tree.

"You are a hopeless wizard!" the
king cried. "Over the side you go!"

"Help!" cried Wizzle. Then he saw Wanda. She was holding a bow and arrow.

Wizzle knew what she was planning.

"Let me try one last spell," he said
to the king.

Wizzle waved his wand. "Take us down to earth!" he shouted.

Just at that moment Wanda shot an arrow. It hit the balloon and hot air began to escape.

The balloon floated gently down
to earth.

The king was delighted. So was
the queen!

"Maybe you're not such a bad
wizard after all," he said, smiling
at Wizzle.

START READING is a series of highly enjoyable books for beginner readers. They have been carefully graded to match the Book Bands widely used in schools. This enables readers to be sure they choose books that match their own reading ability.

The Bands are:

Pink / Band 1
Red / Band 2
Yellow / Band 3
Blue / Band 4
Green / Band 5
Orange / Band 6
Turquoise / Band 7
Purple / Band 8
Gold / Band 9

START READING books can be read independently or shared with an adult. They promote the enjoyment of reading through satisfying stories supported by fun illustrations.

Anne Cassidy has written lots of books for children. Many of them are about talking animals who get into trouble. She has two dogs, Charlie and Dave, but, sadly, neither of them talk to her! This time she wanted to write about a funny wizard who gets his spells mixed up.

Martin Remphry grew up on the tiny Channel Island of Sark. He has always loved drawing, especially spooky things such as witches and wizards, so it was a dream come true for him to illustrate Wizzle. He loves the funny ingredients Wizzle uses for his spells, even if they don't always work as he hopes!